Referability Roadmap

BILL UTNAGE

Referability Roadmap

Quantity sales and special discounts are available on quantity purchases by corporations, associations, and others. For details, contact the publisher at the address above.

Orders by U.S. trade bookstores and wholesalers. Email info@BeyondPublishing. net

The Beyond Publishing Speakers Bureau can bring authors to your live event. For more information or to book an event contact the Beyond Publishing Speakers Bureau speak@BeyondPublishing.net

Illustrations by Bob Eckstein

The Author can be reached directly at BeyondPublishing.net

Manufactured and printed in the United States of America distributed globally by BeyondPublishing.net

New York | Los Angeles | London | Sydney

Library of Congress Control Number:

ISBN Softcover: 978-1-637923-71-9

ISBN Hardcover: 978-1-637923-70-2

For God, the reason for everything good in my life.
For my wife, Joni, my biggest supporter.
For Dale, Becky, and Natalie,
for being great business partners.

ACKNOWLEDGEMENTS

I believe in life we are successful because of the people we surround ourselves with. All the great things in my life have been the result of a relationship.

I want to say thank you to those that have been part of my journey. First and foremost, all glory goes to God, he has been so good to me. To my wife Joni, who always believes in me, even when I don't believe in myself. To my daughter, Amber, who inspires me everyday. My wonderful grandchildren, Hudson, Sloane and Lennon and to my parents.

Thank you to Dean Wieben for giving me my first business opportunity. John Kachoyeanos for being a mentor. Klemmer and Associates for helping change my life and my thinking. Dale and Becky Crane and Natalie Nielsen for being wonderful business partners. Mark Jordan for being my pastor. Craig Duswalt for creating the book writing system that allowed me write this book and Michael Butler, my publisher.

CONTENTS

INTRODUCTION

This book is over 30 years in the making, and I know what you are thinking, shouldn't it be more pages then? My goal with this book is to share with you the key things I have learned in owning and running serviced-based businesses for over 30 years and continue to do so. This book provides you a roadmap, if you follow it, that will help you build and grow an amazing business.

After spending 6 years in the Air Force, I was given an opportunity by my best friend to join him in his chiropractic business where I spent 14 years operating multiple locations with much of the business coming by referral. In 2005, I left the chiropractic world and went into real estate. Since that time, we have built one of the most productive and profitable real estate teams in our area with 95% of the business coming from referrals.

Over the last 30 plus years I have had the opportunity to coach and consult with hundreds of serviced based business owners and help them grow their business through referrals.

I currently own Damascus Road Coaching & Consulting and I am the Florida Regional Partner for Master Networks.

I believe this book will provide you the fundamentals and guidance to help you build and grow your referral-based business!

At the end of each chapter, you will see there is space to write down an action step. I encourage you to use that space to write down one thing from the chapter you will implement in your business and then do it.

Remember, nothing changes if nothing changes! Please use this book to help create the business and life you have always wanted.

To your success!

CHAPTER ONE

IT BEGINS IN THE MIND

Know Your Why

Everything first starts in the mind. As Simon Sinek states, "Start with why." Why do you want to be a business owner? Why do want to build a referral-based business? **This is such an important part of the business process, so don't overlook it.**

It's your why that is going to give you clarity for your business and be the driving force when obstacles get in the way (because they will). When the negative talk starts, and negative people tell you that you shouldn't do it or you should quit, it will be your Why that keeps you going. So, know it and live it!

Growth Mindset

Do you believe that the life you have been dealt is it? That you don't have any control over how your life turns out? Or do you believe that by making better choices and by being willing to learn and grow that you can accomplish more? If you believe the latter, then you have a growth mindset.

To a successful business owner, having a growth mindset is key. We must understand that we can't control most of what happens in our life, but we have full control over our reactions and our effort. We have choice!

Part of that growth mindset is coming from a place of abundance and not scarcity. We must believe that there is enough business, money, etc. Because there is! **When we live with an abundance mindset, we focus on the solutions, not the problems.**

Goals

A goal without a plan is only a dream! As a business owner, we know we will never have the business we want if we don't have a written plan for it. This is what our goals are for….to turn our dream into a reality!

There are many goal-setting systems you can use. The one I have found that works well and that is simple is SMART.

S	-Specific (I want to make $200,000.)

M	-Measurable (Yes, because it is a number.)

A	-Achievable (Can you achieve it? It might be stretch, but you believe you can do it) Side note: If you don't believe you can do it… you won't. I'm all for big goals, but big goals that are never reached leave you feeling that you failed.

R	-Relevant (Is it in line with your overall goal?)

T	-Time-based (I want to achieve my goal by the end of 2022.)

Use this system to filter all your goals through. By doing this, it will give you clarity. Remember to put your goals in writing!

Focus

Focus on what you want…not what you don't want. Remember what we focus on, we get more of that in our lives….. good and bad! So, why not focus on the good?

A key element to focusing is knowing what we want to achieve. As an archer aims for the bullseye, we should know what we are aiming at— if we don't know what it is we are aiming at, we will never hit it.

Our targets, if you will, are our goals. When we are clear on those, then we are more likely to achieve them. As with knowing your Why for your business, so we must know our why for the goals we set.

Another key element for focus is removing the distractions from our lives while we are working towards our goals. We all lead hectic, crazy lives at times, and everything is trying to get our constant attention. So, removing as many distractions as possible will help you focus.

First, time block on your schedule for focused time on your goals. If you don't have a schedule, create one. **If it's not on your schedule, it won't get done!**

Be committed to that time by removing distractions, turning off your phone, email, and social media notifications. Honor that block of time like it is an appointment with a new client.

Know your best energy times for working on your most important things. If you are morning person, then time block in the morning. If you are night owl, then time block at night. Use your energy levels to your favor.

It is very difficult to focus on multiple goals at once. Prioritize your goals, and work on the most important one during your time blocks.

1% Better

Progress not perfection. Remember, you can't change everything in one day. Focus on constant, incremental, improvement. Think about getting one percent better every day, and imagine where you will be by the end of the year!

Practice the Pareto Principal, also know as the 80/20 Rule. The rule states that 20 percent of our work leads to 80 percent of results. The key is knowing what activities are in the 20 percent. As a business owner, I will share with you what I believe they are after over 30 years of owning and operating businesses.

1. Lead generation

2. Lead follow up

Focus on these key activities, and your business will thrive.

Have a plan to get better in all aspects of your life. Your health, relationships, and your finances. **You must be intentional when you want greatness in your life… it doesn't come by chance!**

Personal Responsibility

All the things mentioned above will either be achieved or not achieved based on the choices you make. You can either come from a place of personal responsibility or from a place of being a victim. You get to choose.

The victim viewpoint is where something has been done to you or you have been taken advantage of… you are not in control. This is a weak mindset.

The personal responsibility viewpoint is that you are at cause for your situation based on choices you have made. This is a strong mindset. You take ownership of where you are…good or not so good.

By choosing to come from a place of taking personal responsibility, you get to choose to do something, rather than having to do something.

It's your life…take responsibility for it!

THE ACTION I WILL TAKE

CHAPTER TWO

WHY BUILD A REFERRAL-BASED BUSINESS?

Control Your Time

What is the one thing that all of us have in common? Time, each one of us have 24 hours each day. What makes us different is how we spend those 24 hours.

I believe that time is the most important asset we have. Why? Because we can make more money, but we can't make more time!

With a Referral Based Business (RBB), you have better control of your time. Because you know who you are marketing to, talking to, and spending time with, you are more focused and can make better use of your time.

Instead of showing up each day and wondering who you should contact, market to, and spend time with and chasing lower value customers, **with the RBB, you are spending time with higher value customers, therefore maximizing your time.**

Productivity

By saving time in your RBB, you also have higher productivity! If the old saying "that time is money" is true, then controlling your time should lead to higher productivity.

Since you are marketing to people who already know you and you have a relationship with, your conversion rate should be much higher than with a cold lead. With a cold lead, you must "sell them" or "convince them to work with you."

With the people who already know, like, and trust you, there really isn't any selling. It's giving them guidance and helping them with a problem, because you already have a relationship with them. The speed of trust is much higher, which leads to the process going much smoother and quicker.

Profitability

Profit is key for your business. Without profit, you aren't going to be in business for long.

Because you know who you should be marketing to, you have greater control of your marketing dollars. Think of it as a rifle approach verses a shotgun approach.

With the shotgun approach to marketing, you throw as much stuff out there and see what sticks. You may get lucky and get some return. Or you use the rifle approach, where you aim at specific target (your database) with a message that speaks to them, and since they already know, like, and trust you, your efforts have a much higher potential of return, meaning higher profit!

Because you are doing business with people who know, like and trust you, they can become your unpaid sales force. They can become advocates for your business when they refer their friends and family to you. This is why it's so important to spend more time with the clients who advocate for your business. We will dive deeper into that later in the book.

Just know the more advocates you have, the better and more profitable your business will be!

When you have advocates for your business, and they become your unpaid sales force, it allows you to leverage them, instead of adding more people to your team, which adds to the profitability.

By this, you can strategically build your team to maximize all of the things listed above.

More Fun!

Here's what I have found in over 30 years of business: when you control your time, you have higher productivity, and more profit, the business is a lot more enjoyable and yes…even fun!

This is the beauty of the RBB. When you are working with people who know, like and trust you, the business becomes easier. Don't get me wrong, it's not rainbows and puppy dogs every day, but it's a much better way to operate.

Relationships

Through these relationships, you will find many other benefits other than growing your business.

Because you are working with people who know, like and trust you, you are building relationships and friendships with many of them. Many of my clients have become some of my closest friends. Because of the relationships you are building, other business opportunities may come that otherwise may have not.

You are building a community because you are in consistent contact with your clients. You know what's going on with them and them with you.

You create a sense of purpose. In an RBB, it's more than just money because you are focusing on the people and people matter. The old saying that "no one cares how much you know until they know how much you care" holds true for your business.

More Referrals

When you commit to building an RBB and truly choose to invest in your clients and focus on bringing value to them, it leads to more referrals. The process is simple, not easy.

THE ACTION I WILL TAKE

CHAPTER THREE

THE DATABASE

What is a Database?

First, let's talk about what a database is not. It's not a mailing list. It's not for mass mailings or mass emailing people.

Your database is a relationship list. It is collection of names, addresses, telephone numbers and email addresses of people you know or you have met and want to continue a relationship with or build one.

For an RBB, your database is the lifeblood of your business! Think of it as a living thing. You must feed it, nurture it, and communicate with it. You must constantly engage with it.

What System to Use

You have a collection of all your people. Where do you put them to make connecting with them simple and easy? You will need a CRM(Client Relationship Management system). The system I recommend is the one that you will use. There are literally hundreds of CRMs in the market.

If you already have one that is working for you…wonderful, keep using it! If you don't have one, here are some features to look for.

1. It's easy to use! If it's difficult, you won't use, so don't buy it.
2. It allows you to create categories or tags.
3. It has email capabilities.
4. It has text capabilities.
5. It has the ability to set up reminders/tasks.
6. It has tracking on email open rates.
7. A funnel or landing page builder would be a bonus.

Over the last 30 plus years, I have used many different systems, and the technology continues to improve with more bells and whistles that you may or may not need.

Currently, I use Auto Max for my CRM. It has all the items listed above, plus many more that I may use at some point in the future. Also, they have great customer service.

I have negotiated a special price for you if you would like to use them. Visit AutoMaxCRM.com to check it out. To get your discount contact Bill Davey at Bill@AutoMaxCRM.com and let him know Bill Utnage referred you and you will receive a big discount!

Sorting

So, who goes into your database? Everyone you know that you want to connect with.

- Friends
- Family members
- Clients/customers, past and current
- Business owners
- Neighbors
- People you have just met

Who doesn't go in it? People that you don't like and don't want to connect with. All of us have had those clients or customers that just weren't a good fit. If that's the case, don't put them in. Remember, you are building a relationship list, not a mailing list. If you know that you won't connect with them, let them go.

Now that you know who is going into our database, the next step is to sort them by their worth to your business. Now don't hear what I'm not saying. You are not judging your clients' worth as a person. All of them have worth. What I'm talking about is their worth to your business.

For example, Sarah is past client and is a connector. She consistently refers multiple people to you per year. John, on the other hand, is a past client as well but has only referred one person to you. Which one has greater worth to your business? The answer is Sarah because she has shown that is she is an advocate for your business through the consistent referrals.

You want to sort and categorize your database, so you are strategic in how you communicate with the people who have the most worth to your business. This allows you to maximize your time and increase your productivity, as I outlined in Chapter 2.

I recommended sorting your clients into three categories:

- A-Clients who refer you multiple times a year or do business with you multiple times a year. These are your advocates!
- B-People who have done business with you or have referred at least once. Past and current clients.
- C-People you have met, or you know but haven't done business with yet.

You can use any label, 1, 2, 3 or 5-star, 4-star, 3-star. Just know what each category means to you.

Qualifying

Now that you have everyone in your database, it's time to qualify them. Which means you have them in your database, you have all their contact information, and you have them sorted. The next question is: would they still use you and recommend you?

There is a great script from Brian Buffini that is called the Mayor Campaign.

"Hi John, this is Bill Utnage. If you were thinking about buying or selling a home, or you had a friend or family member who was, would I still be the agent you would refer to?"

If they say yes, say, "Great, I really appreciate your support!" Keep them in your database.

If they say no, ask them why. It's usually because they have a friend or family member who is now in your line of business, and they feel obligated to refer them. Thank them for sharing that with you and let them know if that relationship changes, you are still here for them. Remove them from your database. There is no reason to spend energy and money on those who are not going to do business with you.

Feed it

Make sure you are consistently adding to your database. You can use the Mayor Campaign script on every person you meet—just modify it.

"If you were thinking about buying or selling a home, or you had a friend or family member who was, would you have a real estate agent you would refer to?"

I they say no, say, "Great! I would love to be that agent!"

Ask them if it would be okay if you contacted them from time to time with information that they might find useful. Get their contact information and add them to your database in the C category.

The goal is to move as many people up to the A category as you can.

Also, have weekly goal on how many people you want to add to your database.

Engagement

Now that you sorted and qualified your database, the next step is to engage with it on a consistent basis.

I recommend at least 36 times a year! I know what you are thinking that is way too much, but it's not. Think about how many messages you are receiving daily in the form of email, texts, social media, TV, and radio. You must be consistently in front of your client to be top of mind.

You want to do that with a mixture of mediums. Below is an example of what that might look like.

1. One time per month, a direct piece with something of value (newsletter, market update, discount coupon, etc.).
2. One time per month, an email with something of value.
3. Once per quarter, a check-in phone call.
4. Send them a birthday card.
5. Once per quarter, send them a video text with something of value.
6. Twice a year, send them a handwritten note.
7. Twice a year, have lunch or coffee with them.

Add all that up and it's 37 contacts in a year! Not that hard.

Keep in mind not to rely on all passive contact forms (email and text messages). The best connects are face-to-face or voice-to-voice! That's how you build and deepen relationships and increase referrals.

THE ACTION I WILL TAKE

CHAPTER FOUR

KNOW, LIKE, AND TRUST
SALES IS A CONTACT SPORT

In Chapter 3, I talked about engagement by consistently connecting with your database. In this chapter I want to go deeper into what that looks like to build a relationship with your clients and potential clients. Remember, your database is made up of real people.

As I discussed earlier, to build a relationship that causes people to know, like, and trust you, you must spend time with them. If I only talked to my wife once a month, our marriage probably wouldn't be very strong. Our relationship with our clients is the same. The more contact you have with them and the more value you bring to them, the deeper the relationship and the more valuable you become to them. Because they look at you as friend or a trusted advisor, rather than a salesperson.

To stay in contact with them, you must have a plan. Without a plan, you cannot stay in contact with them on a consistent basis.... and consistency is the key.

Invest Time

In Sorting, I shared with you about categorizing your database based on their value to the business. As I previously shared, face-to-face or voice-to-voice are the two best ways to deepen the relationship. Below shows the suggested connects based on each of the categories. These are the minimums.

- A clients: once a month face-to-face or voice-to-voice
- B clients: every two months face-to-face or voice-to-voice
- C clients: once per quarter face-to-face or voice-to-voice

Remember when you are in conversation with your people, be more interested than interesting. Focus on what's going on with them and how you can help them or bring value. Stay away from "Who do you know that's buying or selling a home that I can help?" Don't get me wrong, if they ask you how they might be able to help you, it's fine to let them know what that looks like. Just don't lead with that. As you deepen a relationship, people will want to help you.

Also, always be looking for ways to bring them value. If they own a business, refer them to your other clients. Send them a book you think they would benefit from, share a podcast, connect them with someone that might be good synergy partner. The more valuable you become in their life…the more valuable they become in yours and your business.

Remember what we appreciate, appreciates!

Be Likeable

The one truth about people is that they ultimately want to do business with people they know, like, and trust. The first step is they must know who you are. Which is the easy part. You meet someone and have a conversation and now, they know you, but only on a superficial level at that point.

The next step is to be likeable. What is your likeability rating? Does the room light up when you walk into it or when you walk out of it? I've heard people say, "I don't care if people like me or not, it's business!" After 30 years of being in the service-based business world, I totally disagree.

Take a moment and think about yourself. Let's say you are looking for a financial advisor and you meet Lisa, who has a great reputation as a financial advisor. During a meeting with her, she only talks about herself and how great she is and all the great things she has accomplished, which may all be true, but she never asks about you or seems interested in who you are. Now, even though she may be great at what she does, are you going to be compelled to do business with her? Probably not. Why? Because she didn't make herself likeable.

It's just human nature: we want to be around people we like and make us feel good. So, work on your likeability rating. As it gets better, so will your business.

Build Trust

I covered the know and like factors, now, let's talk about the trust factor. We meet someone, get to know them, and we like them, now what builds the trust factor?

What doesn't work is saying "trust me." I believe trust is something we earn every day. Here are the things that I believe help build trust:

- Honor your word. If you say you will do it, do it! When you make a mistake, own it. Apologize and make it right, even if it costs you money.

- Listen and ask questions. Be clear on what your client wants. People want to feel heard and understood.

- Show up on time, which means be early. My credo is if you're not 10 minutes early, you're late! I have never lost business because I showed up early. I have lost it because I showed up late.

- Be prepared, even overprepared.

- Under-promise and over-deliver. Don't just meet expectations, exceed them. This is how you get referred.

Remember, everything you do and don't do is always telling a story about who you are. What story are you telling?

Be a Problem Solver

There is a saying that the bigger the problems you can solve, the more you're worth. Meaning if you can only solve small problems in your business, then you will probably only make a small amount of money. This is why a brain surgeon makes more than a bus driver. The brain surgeon is solving much bigger problems.

This is the same for your clients. When you can help them solve their problems, you become more valuable to them. Even if it's not you who can solve it, but you know someone who can.

You do this by focusing on their needs. And the only way to do that is to be in relationship with them.

Be a Connector

As I stated above, you may not be the one who solves your client's problem, but you may know someone who can. This is being a connector. This piece is hugely important and often overlooked.

This is why you want to build a network of allied resources that you can tap into when there is a problem to be solved and you can't solve it yourself. I will go more into the power of your network in a later chapter.

THE ACTION I WILL TAKE

CHAPTER FIVE

THE POWER OF YOUR NETWORK
YOUR NETWORK IS YOUR NET WORTH

In the previous chapters, I have shared with you the importance of having a database of past and current clients as well as new people you meet who haven't done business with you or referred you…yet.

In this chapter, I want to share why it's important to grow your network and some ideas on how to do it.

Why is it so important to grow your network? To grow your business, more people must know you, what you do, and how you do it. It's simple math really… the more people that know you, like you, and trust you, the more opportunities you will have!

As with everything you do in your business, you must have a plan to achieve it. Growing your network is no different.

Be strategic, look at your current network, and see where the gaps are. For example, if you are an insurance agent, you should have a relationship with a great mortgage lender. If you are a mortgage lender, you should have a relationship with a great real estate agent.

When you are clear on who you are looking for, it's much easier to find them. Also, ask yourself who already has the people you're looking for and connect with them. For example, if you are a business coach, join your local chamber of commerce and start making connections there.

Business Networking Groups

One of the best ways to expand your network is to be part of formal business networking group like Master Networks. Master Networks is a national business building and networking organization. Their focus is to help their members build relationships that lead to business growth. They hold weekly one-hour, high-energy meetings with rotating agendas and offer industry exclusivity. I have been part of Master Networks for several years. To find out more, go to www. MasterNetworks.com

Another great option is your local Chamber of Commerce. It's not as good as being in a weekly networking organization, but it can still connect you with people who could be synergy partners for you.

A great group that serves a dual purpose is Toastmasters. This is a public speaking training group. Its members are usually other business owners who are looking to improve their public speaking skills. It is great organization. I spent four years with them and not only improved my speaking ability, but also built some great relationships as well. To find out more, go to www.Toastmasters.org

Another option is online business networking groups, such as Alignable. This online platform allows business owners to connect worldwide. They offer networking and business training. To find out more, go to www.alignable.com

Civic Groups

Civic or service-based groups are a great place to build relationships with like-minded people and give back to your community. Here's just a few of them:

- Rotary
- Kiwanis
- Lions
- Optimist

I have been a member of Rotary for over 15 years and have built friendships and help make changes in my community and the world.

I recommend going and visiting the ones you have interest in and seeing which one is a good fit. Remember, pick one and go deep.

Social/Interest Groups

If you know people want to do business with those they know, like, and trust, then being around people with a common interest is great place to be.

If you are a runner, you could join a running club. People like people who are like them. Here are some ideas for some groups:

- Cooking
- Scuba diving
- Golf
- Tennis
- Book clubs

- Painting
- Military service

The list is almost endless. Find one that you have a genuine interest in and see if it's a fit.

Create Your Own Group

Another great option is to create your own social or interest group. This has several benefits. It's your group, so you get to be in control of it (great for the control freaks). It puts you in the center of it, which makes you the "expert".

I know a real estate agent who created a group that was just for new people who had just moved to the community or were thinking about moving to the community. He has different events each month designed to help people get connected. He is bringing tons of value to those people and making himself valuable to them. His business has grown tremendously from it!

Go Deep, Not Wide

A word of caution! Don't try to do it all…it won't work. As I stated before, go deep, rather than wide. Remember in an RBB, it is about building relationships, which can take time.

What I have experienced to work best is to be in no more than three groups. Pick the groups you really enjoy. If you don't enjoy them and you are just joining for the business, you will ultimately end up leaving.

When you do join, commit to being there consistently, and volunteer for leadership or committees— that's how you build deeper relationships.

THE ACTION I WILL TAKE

CHAPTER SIX

VALUE, VALUE, VALUE

VIP Program

As I have already shared, offering value and being of value to your clients and customers is essential. This can be done in a lot of different ways. In this chapter, I'm going to share some tips on how to increase your value with your clients.

Create a VIP Program. This one of the best ways to create value with your clients. Everyone wants to be a VIP! By having a VIP Program, it's way to reward those who support your business. The beauty about this program is that it can look a lot of different ways.

Here are some ideas for your VIP Program:

- Have a network of vendors to refer them to.
- Host client events.
- Offer a free notary service.
- Run quarterly promotions.
- Offer giveaways.

Be creative and make it a value for your clients.

Discounts

A goods place to start is offering discounts from your vendors and people in your network. Let's say you have a relationship with a carpet cleaning company. Contact them and ask if they would be willing to offer a discount to your clients when they use their services in a particular month. Let's say they offer a 10 percent discount just for your clients for the month of July.

You can contact your database and share with them that because of the relationship you have with the carpet cleaning company, they can get 10 percent off on their carpet cleaning. By doing this, you build value with your clients and customers, plus deepen the relationship with your carpet cleaner.

You can also take this a step further by partnering with the carpet cleaner and having them share in the costs if you are doing this as a direct mail piece.

Reward the behavior.

One the best things you can receive is a referral from someone in your database. When this happens, reward the behavior. Don't wait to see if it turns into business or not; you want to reward the behavior of them making the referral. Because what you reward usually continues.

I recommend sending them a handwritten note thanking them for the referral. Depending on your industry, you may not be able to give something of value, but if you can, send them a small personal gift. I suggest that you don't send them a shirt with your logo on it. Be creative and make it personal. If you know they like red wine, drop a bottle of wine off at their house, send them a book they would enjoy, take them to lunch. Make it personal.

Client Events

One the best ways to increase value for your clients is to host client events. Why this is so powerful is that you are one to many, which is a great leverage of time. It also helps connect your clients with each other.

If you are not currently doing client events, I suggest you start with one and make it a family event. It could be something as small as hosting cookout in a local park and having a bounce house and games for kids and adults.

Another example is in one of my businesses, we host a bowling party each year where we rent an entire bowling alley on a Saturday afternoon for two hours, and our clients get to come and bowl and eat for free! We also do giveaways for prizes and have someone there taking photos of each family that we send to them after the event. Our clients love this, and it "sells out" every year.

Some other ideas for client events:

- Have a donut giveaway.
- Give out pies at Thanksgiving.
- Host a learning event.
- Rent out a movie theater and host a movie night.
- Rent out local pool and have beach party.

Pro tip: Make sure you heavily promote your event. Have a registration page, calls, emails, and texts. The success of your event will be the result of your intentionality of getting people to it.

On the bigger ticket events, you can partner with your vendors to help offset some costs.

Finally, make sure you are at the event. Your presence is must. You can't build relationships if you aren't there.

Keep in mind that these client events are an investment in your business. Once you have one event down, you can build on that and then add another.

Be a Trusted Advisor

Another way to bring value is to make sure your clients know that you are dedicated to working in their best interest. I know this sounds obvious, but sometimes business owners lose sight of their clients' needs by focusing just on the money. Focus on the client, and the money will come.

Guard your Reputation

The Will Rogers quote, "It takes a lifetime to build a good reputation, but you can lose it in a minute" is true. Your greatest asset is your reputation. That's how you will get referred or not get referred. By focusing on building a reputation of honoring your word, putting your clients first, and doing the right thing, you are bringing value to them.

THE ACTION I WILL TAKE

CHAPTER SEVEN

THE SECRET SAUCE-CONSISTENCY

Have a System

Over the last 30 plus years of owning and operating businesses, when asked what is the key to the RBB success, I say being consistent in everything you do. Be consistent in your marketing, your lead generation, your lead follow up, your mindset, absolutely everything.

Here's why: because most businesses aren't. They try out the marketing system of the month or do something for a couple of months, and then, they say it didn't work. You want to be boringly consistent.

To have consistency in your business, you must have systems and processes in place. Without having these, things are just thrown on the wall to see what sticks.

Have a communication plan, as I shared in Chapter 3, know who and when you are going to communicate with your clients. That's why it's vital that your CRM allows you to categorize your clients and is able to set up action plans. The more you can automate this process, the better. The easier we make it, the more likely it will get done.

Marketing Plan

Once you know who and when you are connecting with, now you need to know what you are going to communicate. This is where having a marketing calendar comes in. Know your message each month or your theme. For example, let's say you are a residential real estate agent, and you want to increase your listing inventory. And in your area, January is the month people start thinking about selling their home. You would create marketing messages that would go out to your database geared around getting your home ready to sell.

So, for the month of January, your messaging is focused on attracting people who want to sell their home. Then, in February, it might be sharing with your database the benefits of building a home. If you do that for each month of the year, you have talking points and specific messaging for your business through the whole year. This helps with your consistency.

Marketing Calendar

Now that you know what you are going to say and to who, the next step is to put it in writing through your marketing calendar.

Your marketing calendar should be in writing and have your entire year of messaging laid out. This means your telephone conversation topics, emails, text messages, and social media posts. Everything you are messaging out should have consistent messaging based on your marketing calendar.

Also, your marketing calendar should reflect who is responsible for handling each aspect. For example, if you have someone who handles your social media, make sure they have the marketing calendar and they know their role. If you are doing it all yourself (bad idea, by the way, and I will share more about that in upcoming chapter), then you have to be clear on the schedule of the messaging. Again, be thinking about consistency.

Have a Goal

What action do you want your clients or prospects to take with the information you are providing them? Make sure you have a call to action. As an insurance agent, you could have a special report about the 10 best ways to save money on your car insurance. And the goal might be to have 20 or more people download or request the report. The clearer you are on what you want to happen, the more likely it is to happen.

You goal could be:

- Number of leads.
- Number of appointments scheduled.
- Number of sales.
- Adding new people to your database.

The good news is that you get to set the goals that work for you. Remember, it's not a goal if it's not written down…it's only a wish.

Wash, Rinse, Repeat

There is a term called the stacking effect. What it means is that it's not just one thing done once that leads to a result. It is many things done over time. We make a call to a client, we send them a handwritten note, they come to an event, they read a direct mail piece you sent, they see a social media post. It is the stacking of each of those things that leads to an action. This is where the consistency comes in. The stacking effect is built by consistency.

Here's the challenge with your business: most of the time, you don't know when a client or prospect will need or want your services. This is why you consistently connect with them through different mediums and with different messages, so that when they have a need, you are there.

This is the beauty of the stacking affect. I have had past clients connect with me after 10 years because I consistently stayed in contact with them. I was able to do that because I had a system for it.

Don't overthink it!

A word of caution to the perfectionists who are reading this book. It will never be perfect, the system, the marketing piece, the message, none of it! I know that's hard to read. I want you to think progress, not perfection. If you wait until it's perfect, you will miss a lot of opportunities.

I want you to think GETMO-Good Enough To Move On. Is it 90 percent of what you want? If so, move on. You can always tweak things as you are going and as you get feedback. If you never send anything out, then nothing can work.

CHAPTER EIGHT

PROFIT

Know Your Numbers

In Chapter 2, I talked about profitability being a benefit of having an RBB. In this chapter, I'm going to drill down on what you need to track and do to ensure that your business is profitable.

One of the biggest challenges that I see with business owners is consistently tracking their key metrics in their business. Remember what you don't track you can't measure.

Here are the eight key numbers you must track in your business:

- The number of leads that are coming into the business.
- The number of appointments set from those leads.
- The number sales.
- Conversion rates.
- Income into the business.
- Expenses for the business.
- Gross and net profit.
- Number of people in the database.

By tracking these numbers, you will know the health of your business at all times.

Conversion Rates

So, now that you know the key numbers to track, let's drill down and get clearer on how to make the numbers better. You do this by knowing your conversion rates.

Here the three key conversion rate equations:

- The number of contacts to get a lead.
- The number of leads to get an appointment.
- The number of appointments to get a sale.

For example, if you know that it takes ten contacts to get one lead/referral and it takes two leads/referrals to get one appointment and two appointments to get one sale, you can create your goals numbers with more accuracy.

By knowing your conversion rates, you can change your results by knowing where you need to improve a certain skill set. For example, if you reduce the number of contacts needed to get a lead/referral to five, instead of ten, then your results would increase. It is the same way with leads to appointments and appointments to sales.

Knowing these numbers is freeing, because you can follow a formula that will give you a result, instead of guessing or hoping that you have done enough lead generation. Now you will know based on results!

The Accounts

You are running a business, so treat it as such. Keep the money your business makes separate from your personal money. You do this by having separate bank accounts for your business.

Here are the basic accounts you need:

- Business operating account
- Tax account
- Capital account

Your business operating account is where all the money your business generates goes into and where all the expenses are paid out of.

The tax account. Since you are a business owner, you are more than likely going to be responsible for paying all your own taxes. Please consult with a CPA to find the best tax structure for your business. Make sure you are setting aside the right amount of money to cover your taxes.

The capital account. This account is used for improvements in your business, such as new computers, software, furniture, etc. You can determine the appropriate amount you feel you may need for future projects.

By having this separation of accounts, it is much easier and more accurate to track the TRUE profit of your business.

Profit and Loss Statement

The Profit and Loss Statement or the P&L shows the health of your business and is a must to have. It will reflect all the money that came in and all the money that went out and what it was spent on.

If you are handling your own books, then make sure you are using some sort of accounting software, such as Quickbooks. This will save you a tremendous amount of time and provide you with a P&L Statement, as well as many other useful tools. If you are using a bookkeeping service or CPA to handle your accounts, make sure you are reviewing your P&L every month.

Also, creating a budget for your business is wise as well. This allows you to hold your money accountable.

Have Advisors

There are a lot of things as a business owner you must know, or you must know the person that knows. Having the right advisors in your business is imperative to running a successful business.

Here are the key advisors I believe you should have:

- Certified Public Accountant (CPA)
- Attorney
- Insurance agent
- Business coach

Don't look at these advisors as an expense, look at them as an asset to your business. When you have the right ones, your life and business should be much better.

Take Ownership

This is your business, so take ownership of it. The beauty of being a business owner is that you get to direct where it goes. With the right people and systems, you can build it however you choose.

Make sure you are working in your 20 percent, as we discussed earlier. Don't be doing $15 an hour work if you are worth $100 an hour.

Don't be afraid to ask for help. No one can know it all, and the sooner you realize that, the better your business will be. Ask yourself, do I want to be right, or do I want to be profitable? Sometimes, we don't get both.

CHAPTER NINE

LEVERAGE

Know Your Worth

There is a saying "If you want to go fast, go alone. If you want to go far, go with a team." Operating your business works the same. If you want to grow or scale your business, you are going to need help. In this chapter, I am going share with you why and how to do that.

There is one thing that all of us have in common. Do you know what that is? Time, everyone has the same 24 hours in a day. What makes each of us different is how we spend those 24 hours.

As a business owner, you have to know what your time is worth per hour. You do that by dividing your income by the number of hours worked. Let's say you made $100,000 last year, and you worked approximately 2,000 hours. Your dollar per hour rate would be $50.

Why is this number important? Because if you are worth $50 an hour and you are doing $15 an hour work in your business, you are losing $35 an hour! Let's say you are spending 10 hours a week replying to email, basic paperwork, etc., that you could hire a part-time assistant to do for $15 an hour. This would free up 40 hours a month for you to focus on higher-income-producing tasks, generating more income that should easily pay for your assistant plus make you more profit.

This is why leverage is so important. It is a way for you to get more out of your 24 hours by leveraging someone else's 24 hours.

Identify the Gap

When you start to look at where you need leverage in your business, identify the gap. Ask yourself, what things am I doing that someone else can do better than me and for less money? Also, what things are you doing that you don't like doing? And if you had someone doing those things, would it allow you to work more in your strength?

When you have a business where everyone is working in their strengths, you will see amazing things happen! So, identify that gap in your business. In my experience, it is usually an administrative position. Having someone who is detailed-oriented to take care of the paperwork, the follow-up, etc.

In your business, it may be someone to handle your marketing, another salesperson, or a bookkeeper. A place to start is to create a Missing Person Report. You do this by writing down what role you need to fill the gap. Let's say it is an administrative assistant. You would write down everything you would want that person to do for your business. Be specific—the more specific, the better. Now, write the qualities you would want that person to have. For example, high integrity, punctuality, attention to detail, team player, etc.

By having all these things written down, you know what you are looking for. And when you know what you are looking for, it's much easier to find it.

You can now take your Missing Person Report and create an ad in a job search platform, share it with your database, and share it with your friends and colleagues to help you find the right person for the position.

Another tool that is a must when you are looking to add to your team is using a behavioral assessment. My favorite is the DISC Assessment. I like this one because it's simple to understand. I recommend before you interview a candidate that you have them take the assessment first to make sure that the job they would be doing is good fit for who they are. If not, you may be trying to put a square peg in a round hole.

Hire for Attitude, not Skillset

So many times, we hire someone based solely on their skillset, and we overlook their mindset. What I mean by this is their attitude and how they react and think is hugely important. They may be great at the job, but if they aren't a team player, or they are highly emotional, this can cause an issue with other team members and lead to tension and bring more issues for you.

Skillset can be taught; attitude cannot. Now, we want someone who does have the skills to do the job, but I would encourage you to make sure they have the right mindset for your organization. As the old saying goes, "One bad apple can spoil the bunch."

Culture

What is the culture of your business? By knowing this, it will help you attract the right people to your team. Because it's your business, you are the culture creator. This goes back to Chapter 1, where I shared about knowing your Why. Knowing your Why helps you create your culture. When you know what your business culture is, it makes it easier to identify the right people for your team.

You can use your culture to filter candidates through. Ask yourself, does this person fit into our culture? If not, don't hire them.

Another aspect of using your culture when adding team members is to have others on your team meet with the candidate. This is something I have done for years in my business. Because the person is already on your team and knows the culture, they can give you feedback on if they feel the candidate would be a good fit for the team or not. There is wisdom in a multitude of counselors.

Hiring Options

I shared about identifying the Who to fill the gap. Now let's look at what are some of the options of the Who. What I mean by this, is how much time do you need them? For example, using the administrative assistant as a Who, do you need them full-time or part-time? You will have to determine the workload for the position. In the beginning, it may be 20 hours a week. And as the business grows, you may move them to a full-time position.

Another option is having a virtual employee. This has become more popular since the pandemic. Our business had a virtual assistant for six years, and one of the businesses I'm a partner in currently has one, and it works great.

Contract labor is another great option. If you are needing certain projects done that might not require part- or full-time employees, utilizing online platforms like Fiverr to get one-off projects done can be very cost-effective.

Hire Slow, Fire Fast

In my experience, the hiring process is what most business owners like doing the least. Because, like me, they aren't good at it, so they put it off until the pain is so high they have to.

I encourage you not to wait until you must have someone today or your business is going to blow up. Get ahead of it. Do your due diligence. Do the work on the front end, and it will save you on the backend.

If you will utilize the Missing Person Report, know your culture, hire for attitude, and use a behavioral assessment, these things will make the process much easier.

Also, listen to your gut. Most of the time it is right; that's why they call it the second brain.

The bottom line is, to grow your business, you will need help, and the easier you make the process, the better it is for you and your business.

THE ACTION I WILL TAKE

CHAPTER TEN

DO IT NOW!

Fear

One of the greatest challenges that we face, not only as business owners but as human beings is fear, which leads to worry. Fear and worry are thieves; they rob you of all the greatness in your life and business. They are liars, they tell us that we can't do it or shouldn't do it. They rob us of our joy and keep us in our comfort zone.

If you are letting fear keep you from stepping out of your comfort zone, I challenge you to feel the fear but step out anyway. Because on the other side of fear is FREEDOM!

Research has shown that less that 10 percent of the things we fear or worry about actually happen, and when they do, they are not as nearly as bad as we built them up that they would be.

Don't hear what I'm not saying, I'm not saying to live reckless and put your life and business in danger. What I am saying is that don't let fear and worry keep you from doing something that could make your life or business better because you are unsure of how it will turn out.

There are two words that I want to share about letting fear and worry control your life….STOP IT!

Speed is the Great Separator

One of the keys to any successful business is the speed of implementation. Your business will only benefit when you actually implement something different into it. The longer you wait to do that, the less likely you will ever do it.

As I stated before, it's progress, not perfection. Remember, GETMO, Good Enough To Move On? While you are waiting to get it perfect, the competition is getting ahead. Move the needle each day!

Accountability

The old saying goes, "Everyone wants accountability until they get it!" If that is how you feel about accountability, then I think you are missing the power of it.

By being accountable to someone or something, it raises your intention and awareness about it. This is why having an accountability partner or a coach is so important in your business.

Because when you are just accountable to you, it's easy to let yourself off the hook. We come up with tons of excuses for why things aren't happening the way we want them to. When we have others we are accountable to, it's difficult not to take ownership of your choices.

When you have the right accountability partner or coach, they should be holding you capable of what you say you want. They should not be creating your goals, just supporting you around them.

Invest in Your Business

I believe your business is your greatest asset. It's what you know and what you can control. You can't control the stock market, government policy, inflation, the list goes on. You can control what goes on with your business, though.

This is why investing in your business is imperative. Your business is either growing or dying; it never stays static. Always be looking at what you need that will help you grow or be more efficient or profitable. It could be new technology or a new software system, increasing your marketing budget, hiring. Find out what that is and invest in it.

Invest in Yourself

Your business will grow to the extent of your personal growth. Read that again. Because it's true. When you stop learning and growing as a person, I believe it has a direct impact on your business.

Statistically only about three percent of business owners will invest in themselves in such things a going to conferences, taking a class, or self-improvement. So just by reading this book, you are in the top three percent! Congratulations!

I know I have already stated this several times throughout the book, but I can't stress the importance of having the accountability partner or better yet, hiring a coach. Our business changed dramatically when we hired a business coach.

Because what you pay for, you pay attention to. And by having someone who is trained to see what you may be missing and to hold you capable of what you say you want, is worth every penny.

Surround yourself with other like-minded people. Being part of a mastermind is a another great way to invest in yourself. There is wisdom in a multitude of counselors. If you can't find a mastermind to join, create one.

Nothing Changes if Nothing Changes

In the last 9 chapters, I have shared a lot of information that right now is just head knowledge, ideas, strategies, and tactics. Now, you get to choose what you are going to do with the information. If you just keep it in your head, nothing will change.

If knowledge about something was enough, then, as Brian Klemmer states, "Everyone would be skinny, rich, and happy!" It's not the just the knowledge, it's putting knowledge to action. This is how change happens!

Focus on what you want in your life and business, not what you don't want. I challenge you to take one step each day towards that goal, and success is inevitable! Do it now!

THE ACTION I WILL TAKE

MY TOP 10 BUSINESS BOOKS

The Bible
Start with Why   – Simon Sinek
Fierce Conversations   – Susan Scott
Atomic Habits   - James Clear
Think and Grow Rich   – Napolean Hill
The Speed of Trust   - Stephen M. R. Covey
The Compound Effect   - Darren Hardy
The Go Giver   - Bob Burg
The Compassionate Samurai   – Brian Klemmer
*One Small Step Can Change
Your Life: The Kaizen Way*   – Robert Maurer

BONUS BOOKS

Never Split the Difference   – Chris Voss
Winning the War in Your Mind   – Craig Groeschel
The Power of Positive Thinking   – Norman Vincent Peale
*How to Win Friends and
Influence People*   – Dale Carnegie
The Richest Man in Babylon   – George S. Clason

BONUS RESOURCES

Free downloadable resources that will help you put the power
of the Referability Roadmap to work in your business

Go to:

ReferabilityRoadmap.com